FOLLOW THAT FOOD CHAIN

A NILE RIVER Food Chain

A WHO-EATS-WHAT Adventure

Rebecca Hogue Wojahn   Donald Wojahn

Lerner Publications Company
Minneapolis

For Eli and Cal. We hope this answers some of your questions.

There are many links in the chain that created this series. Thanks to Ann Kerns, Kitty Creswell, Carol Hinz, Danielle Carnito, Sarah Olmanson, Paul Rodeen, the staff of the L. E. Phillips Memorial Public Library, and finally, Katherine Hogue

Lerner Publications Company
A division of Lerner Publishing Group, Inc.
241 First Avenue North
Minneapolis, MN 55401 U.S.A.

Website address: www.lernerbooks.com

Library of Congress Cataloging-in-Publication Data

Wojahn, Rebecca Hogue.
   A Nile River food chain : a who-eats-what adventure / by Rebecca Hogue
Wojahn and Donald Wojahn.
      p.   cm. — (Follow that food chain)
   Includes bibliographical references and index.
   ISBN 978–0–8225–7614–3 (lib. bdg. : alk. paper)
   1. Food chains (Ecology)—Egypt—Nile River Delta—Juvenile literature.
I. Wojahn, Donald. II. Title.
QH195.E4W65 2010
577.6′4160962—dc22   2008056142

Manufactured in the United States of America
1 2 3 4 5 6 – BP – 15 14 13 12 11 10

Contents

Introduction
WELCOME TO THE NILE RIVER

The water plants grow so thick along the green, swampy edge of the Nile that it's almost hard to tell there's a river behind them. But there is. The Nile River is the longest river in the world. This part of the Nile is in the northeast corner of Africa. Here, the Nile fans out into what is called the **delta**. Little rain falls in the delta region, but the river brings life to the area.

People have been farming the Nile River delta for more than five thousand years. But big changes have occurred in the last century. In the 1960s, the Aswan High Dam was built on the Nile. The dam stopped the annual floods by holding the water back in an artificial lake, Lake Nasser.

The dam gave Egyptians more water and electrical power. But the dam has changed the river's **habitats**. The yearly floods once washed rich new dirt to the delta. Without the floodwaters, the farmland's soil is poorer. More fertilizer is used. Some of the fertilizer washes into waterways, adding to the region's pollution.

The Nile once had many river branches fanning out from the main river. In between the branches lay marshy, swampy areas. After the dam was built, only two river branches remained. The marshes and swamps have dried out. The birds, frogs, and insects that lived in these areas have lost their home.

Still, there are places tucked away where the papyrus grows tall and millions of birds call, frogs peep, and fish splash. Come meet just a few of the Nile's plants and animals here in this book.

4

MEDITERRANEAN SEA

N

Delta region

EGYPT

Nile River

Aswan
High Dam

Lake
Nasser

RED SEA

5

Choose a
TERTIARY CONSUMER

All the living things in the Nile River delta are necessary for its health and survival. From the swamp cat prowling the shore to the common reed frog singing its song, all living things are connected. Animals and other organisms feed on and transfer energy to one another. This is called a **food chain** or a **food web**.

In food chains, the strongest **predators** are called **tertiary consumers**. They hunt other animals for food and have few natural enemies. Some of the animals they eat are called **secondary consumers**. Secondary consumers are also predators. They hunt plant-eating animals. Plant eaters are **primary consumers**.

Plants are **producers**. Using energy from the sun, they produce their own food. Plants take in **nutrients** from the soil. They also provide nutrients to the animals that eat them.

Decomposers are insects or bacteria (tiny living things) that break down dead plants and animals. Decomposers change them into the nutrients found in the soil.

The plants and animals in a food chain depend on one another. Sometimes there's a break in the chain, such as one type of animal dying out. This loss ripples through the rest of the habitat.

Begin your journey through the Nile River delta food web by choosing a large **carnivore** (meat eater). These tertiary consumers are at the top of the food chain. That means that, for the most part, they don't have any enemies in the cloud forest (except for humans).

When it's time for the tertiary consumer to eat, pick its meal and flip to that page. As you go through the book, don't be surprised if you backtrack and end up where you never expected to be. That's how food webs work—they're complicated. And watch out for those dead ends! When you hit one of those, you have to go back to page 7 and start over with another tertiary consumer.

The main role a plant or animal plays in the Nile River food web is identified by a color-coded shape. Here is the key to that code:

TERTIARY CONSUMER

PRODUCER

SECONDARY CONSUMER

DECOMPOSER

PRIMARY CONSUMER

To choose . . .

. . . a swamp cat, TURN TO PAGE 8.
. . . a black kite, TURN TO PAGE 22.
. . . a Nile crocodile, TURN TO PAGE 31.
. . . a Nile monitor, TURN TO PAGE 34.
. . . a golden jackal, TURN TO PAGE 44.
. . . an Egyptian vulture, TURN TO PAGE 50.

To learn more about a Nile River food web, GO TO PAGE 25.

SWAMP CAT *(Felis chaus)*

The swamp cat stalks through the thick reeds. She is about the size and shape of a house cat, but she's definitely not tame. Her feet barely make a sound in the shallow, muddy water, and her golden brown color blends right in.

The cat's keen eyes catch a slight movement in the water. A frog freezes near the edge of a lily pad. The swamp cat's ears twitch. She crouches. Then—splash! She leaps. But the frog scoots under the water lilies, and the swamp cat comes up empty.

Still hungry, the swamp cat ventures out deeper. She swims over a deep patch and then wades up the other side. The water is clearer here. The cat waits, watching the glimmer of fish in the river. Pow! She shoots her paw out and scoops a fish out of the water.

With the fish flapping in her mouth, the cat brings it to shore. She's just about to dig in when she hears a growl. A golden jackal pokes his head through the riverbank's underbrush. He wants the swamp cat's fish.

The cat drops the fish, ready to fight. To make herself look bigger, she arches her back. The fur on her shoulders stands straight up. She hisses a warning. But the jackal keeps coming.

Not Your Ordinary House Cat

Swamp cats look a little like regular house cats. And, in fact, for a long time, people believed that swamp cats were the ancestors of the cats we keep as pets. That turned out to be untrue. But while swamp cats weren't pets, they were popular with ancient Egyptians. The cats killed poisonous snakes and rats. And in return, the ancient Egyptians never harmed the cats. In fact, Egyptians often mummified (preserved the dead bodies of) cats. Cat mummies have been found in the ancient tombs and pyramids of important people, including pharaohs (Egyptian kings).

The jackal presses closer and bares his teeth. The cat holds her ground and slashes out a paw. As the two circle around each other, the forgotten fish makes its escape. With a couple of flops, the fish flips back into the safety of the river.

Too late, the cat makes a lunge for it. But the fish is gone. The cat stares after it. So does the jackal. Without the fish to fight over, the jackal slinks back into the brush.

The cat paces along the shore, her nose twitching. She watches for a while to see if the fish will surface again. But it doesn't. She'll have to find something else for her meal tonight.

Just as she heads out to hunt again, her ears prick up.
A bark. No, it's not another jackal. It's the call of a male swamp cat, looking for a mate. The female cat hesitates. She's hungry. But the idea of company is welcome too.

She calls back. And she sets off through the reeds to find the male. Good thing she ate not that long ago. **Last night for dinner, the swamp cat chomped . . .**

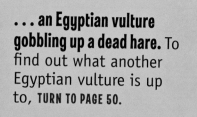

. . . an Egyptian vulture gobbling up a dead hare. To find out what another Egyptian vulture is up to, TURN TO PAGE 50.

. . . a boomslang sunning himself on a log. To find out what another boomslang is up to, TURN TO PAGE 54.

. . . a Nile tilapia speared with the cat's claws. To find out what another Nile tilapia is ups to, TURN TO PAGE 58.

. . . two baby Nile monitors that just crawled out of their eggs. To find out what another Nile monitor is up to, TURN TO PAGE 34.

. . . a black kite chick left alone too long in its nest. To find out what another black kite is up to, TURN TO PAGE 22.

. . . a greater Egyptian gerbil sneaking to the water for a drink. To find out what another greater Egyptian gerbil is up to, TURN TO PAGE 26.

. . . a newly hatched Nile crocodile. To find out what another Nile crocodile is up to, TURN TO PAGE 31.

. . . an Egyptian slit-faced bat that swooped too low chasing a mosquito. To find out what another Egyptian slit-faced bat is up to, TURN TO PAGE 37.

STRIPED HYENA *(Hyaena hyaena)*

In the dark of night, you can hear the striped hyena tear into the deer **carcass**. Not much flesh is left on the carcass, but the hyena finds enough for a meal. Her powerful jaws are stronger than any other mammal her size. She crunches through bones and swallows the hooves whole. She'll eat just about anything.

In fact, as she finishes up the deer, she finds she's still hungry. So she heads to one of her favorite spots—a garbage dump near a small village. She jogs the 3 miles (5 kilometers) there, zigzagging back and forth, just in case she comes across anything else to eat. Her movements look jerky, as if she's limping. Don't worry—she's not hurt. All hyenas' front legs are much longer than their back ones.

Ah, finally. Her ears lead her to the pile of trash outside the village. Other hyenas are here, but there is plenty for all. The

13

village dumps their garbage just for hyenas and other **scavengers**. She digs in, munching down rotten melons, corn, and other leftover bits. In some ways, hyenas are useful to people, always cleaning up the trash.

After a few minutes, she pauses. She hunches and heaves. She spits up a pellet. Pellets are wet wads of food that even hyenas can't digest. This pellet is made up of the hair and bits of hooves from the deer.

She takes a few more bites, but the sun is coming up. It's time to head back home to the burrow for a good day's sleep.

Last night for dinner, the striped hyena gnawed on . . .

. . . **figs and dates that have fallen off the trees.** To learn more about the trees and bushes of the Nile River, TURN TO PAGE 28.

. . . **a black kite that died because her wing was broken.** To find out what another black kite is up to, TURN TO PAGE 22.

. . . **scarab beetles found near a dead Nile monitor.** To find out what another scarab beetle is like, TURN TO PAGE 32.

. . . **an Egyptian tortoise that died because it got stuck on its back.** To find out what another Egyptian tortoise is up to, TURN TO PAGE 51.

. . . **a dead swamp cat.** To find out what another swamp cat is up to, TURN TO PAGE 8.

. . . **an Egyptian vulture that ate poison.** The poison won't bother the tough hyena. To find out what another Egyptian vulture is up to, TURN TO PAGE 50.

. . . **a golden jackal that died of starvation without her mate to help her hunt.** To find out what another golden jackal is up to, TURN TO PAGE 44.

WHITE-HEADED DUCK *(Oxyura leucocephala)*

15

Uh-oh. Do you see those dump trucks and graders over there on the shores of the river? That equipment is bringing loads of sand to fill in the marshy area along the river. Once it's filled in, buildings will be built here. But these shallow, weedy waters are where the white-headed ducks love to paddle, nest, and dive for food. With the shallows filled in, the ducks have one less place to live along the river. The disappearance of white-headed ducks' favorite places to live has made them **endangered**. And that is why this is a *DEAD END*.

PAPYRUS *(Cyperus papyrus)*

The papyrus plants shade the edge of the river. Their roots are snug in the river bottom. Their thick stems stretch overhead as tall as a room's ceiling. At the tops of the stems are "feather dusters"—shoots that stick out all over the place. Flying birds flit in and out between the thick stems. They build nests, peck at the nutty papyrus seeds, and munch on swarms of insects. Swimming birds nibble at the papyrus roots and stems.

Once, papyrus plants were plentiful in the delta. They grew so thick in places that it was impossible to get through the water in a boat. These papyrus swamps were called sudd. But papyrus plants have become much harder to find. That's because the Aswan High Dam was built upstream.

The dam keeps the flow of the river steady and prevents the flooding that used to happen each year. But it was this yearly flooding that made the swamps that papyrus plants love to grow in. Now there's much less space for papyrus plants on the river.

Last night for dinner, the papyrus soaked up . . .

Valuable Papyrus

The papyrus plant was an important part of the lives of ancient Egyptians. They ate parts of it for food, they used it as medicine, and they built boats, shelter, shoes, and decorations with it. But their most valuable use of the papyrus plant was learning how to make paper with it. This creation of paper changed how ancient people communicated and kept information.

. . . **sunshine.** To learn how plants use sunshine, TURN TO PAGE 28.

. . . **nutrients in the soil under the water from poop from a greater flamingo.** To find out what another greater flamingo is up to, TURN TO PAGE 40.

. . . **nutrients in the soil under the water from dead water lilies and lotuses.** To learn more about the water lilies and lotuses of the Nile, TURN TO PAGE 56.

. . . **nutrients in the soil under the water from poop from a great white pelican.** To find out what another great white pelican is up to, TURN TO PAGE 18.

. . . **nutrients in the soil under the water from a dead Egyptian tortoise.** To find out what another Egyptian tortoise is up to, TURN TO PAGE 51.

. . . **nutrients in the soil under the water from dead tree leaves and fruit.** To learn more about the trees and bushes around the Nile, TURN TO PAGE 28.

GREAT WHITE PELICAN *(Pelecanus onocrotalus)*

The great white pelican stretches his wings wide—8 feet (2.4 meters) wide! He skims the river's surface. In a horseshoe shape around him, nine other pelicans do the same. Their flight stirs the fish up. The fish swim hard to stay ahead of the pelicans. Too bad the pelicans have it all planned out.

The fish find themselves in the shallow waters on the edge of the river. This is just where the pelicans want them. Our pelican plunges his bill in the water and scoops up fish with his pouch. With a quick tip forward and then back, the pelican drains the water from his pouch and gulps down the fish whole. It's only nine o'clock in the morning and he's already done eating for the day.

He spends the next hour standing on a sandbar in the river. He preens, picks, and smoothes his feathers. Then he returns home. Home is a nest of twigs, feathers, and grass on the ground. His mate eagerly awaits his arrival. She's been watching their chick. But now that her mate's home, she can go get her own breakfast.

The chick has been waiting for his father's return too. The chick pecks at dad's beak. The father opens his bill wide. The chick sticks his head inside and pulls out bits of the fish the pelican caught earlier.

Last night for dinner, the great white pelican tossed down . . .

Pelicans have been accused of harming the fishing industry. But pelicans actually prefer types of fish that are not wanted by human fishers.

... fish and more fish, such as the Nile tilapia. To find out what another Nile tilapia is up to, TURN TO PAGE 58.

... a common reed frog in the wrong place at the wrong time. To find out what another common reed frog is up to, TURN TO PAGE 47.

Pelican Pouch

Pelicans are best known for their bright yellow pouches. While they do use their pouches to catch fish, they don't store the fish in there for long. Instead, they swallow them down whole. Pelicans do use their pouches for display when mating and when it gets really dry out. Sometimes you can see a pelican standing in the rain with his bill open. He's collecting the rainwater to drink.

LEECHES
(Hirudinoidea)

The baby leeches burst out of their cocoon. Last spring, their parent hid the cocoon in a safe place under a sunken log. Now, smaller than pencil shavings, the babies wiggle out into the shallows of the river. The bottom of the river here is murky and dark with dead leaves. It's the perfect place for baby leeches to find food. The dark depths also keep the leeches hidden from predators.

One by one, the tiny leeches drift apart. They'll live their entire lives underwater. They breathe oxygen through their skins. One leech squirms its way onto a duck. The duck's mate dives and slurps down five other leeches. A different leech snags a frog as it rests in the muck. Another leech latches onto fish.

The leech's sucker sticks to the fish's back. Behind the sucker, teeth gnaw a tiny hole in the fish's scales and skin. The leech sucks down the fish's blood. Special substances in the leech's spit keep the fish from feeling the leech. The spit also keeps the blood from the wound flowing. The leech will stay on the fish until the leech is too full of blood to hang on. It can drink several times its own weight in blood before letting go.

Last night for dinner, the leech drank the blood of...

20

Leech Medicine?

For thousands of years, people have put leeches on sick patients to "bleed" them. People believed that leeches would suck out bad blood and help get rid of illnesses. Most of the time, this didn't work. The loss of blood only made the patients weaker. But more recently, leeches have been used in other ways. Those special substances in leeches' spit are turning out to be very useful. Doctors use them to keep the blood flowing for patients who have had body parts (such as fingers or arms) reattached after an accident. The constant flow of blood keeps the injured part healthy as it heals.

. . . **a greater flamingo sifting the bottom of the river.** To find out what another greater flamingo is up to, TURN TO PAGE 40.

. . . **a purple swamphen nibbling in the reeds.** To find out what another purple swamphen is up to, TURN TO PAGE 52.

. . . **a great white pelican floating on the water.** To find out what another great white pelican is up to, TURN TO PAGE 18.

. . . **a white-headed duck diving for leeches.** To find out what another white-headed duck is up to, TURN TO PAGE 15.

. . . **a Nile tilapia cruising the river bottom.** To find out what another Nile tilapia is up to, TURN TO PAGE 58.

. . . **a Nile monitor resting in the sun.** To find out what another Nile monitor is up to, TURN TO PAGE 34.

. . . **a common reed frog hiding under a lily pad.** To find out what another frog is up to, TURN TO PAGE 47.

BLACK KITE *(Milvus migrans)*

The black kite spreads his wings wide and soars over the river. The length from the tip of one wing to the tip of the other is called a bird's wingspan. The black kite's wingspan is wider than you are tall.

Up here he can see for miles—the river, the sand, and a road twisting nearby. He glides over the road and then circles back down. Something dead lies on the side of the road. He can see an Egyptian vulture eating the **carcass** of some animal. The kite flies lower. He lands and pushes his way in. The vulture retreats, waiting for the bigger bird to finish. The kite rips off a bit of the animal with his yellow hooked beak.

A low rumble can be heard off in the distance. It's coming closer. But the kite doesn't look up. He's used to being one of the area's top predators. He isn't scared of much. The noise grows louder.

A truck roars toward the kite and the hyena. Still the kite doesn't move. At the last second, the truck swerves. The wind of it passing ruffles the kite's brown feathers. He flaps a little but keeps eating. He doesn't even know how close he came to getting killed.

Last night for dinner, the black kite ate . . .

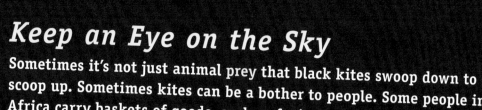

Keep an Eye on the Sky

Sometimes it's not just animal prey that black kites swoop down to scoop up. Sometimes kites can be a bother to people. Some people in Africa carry baskets of goods, such as fruits and vegetables, on top of their heads. Black kites are known to dive down and nab things right out of these baskets. They also sometimes visit picnics and help themselves to the humans' lunch or dinner.

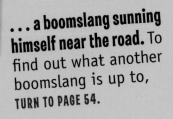

. . . a greater Egyptian gerbil caught out in the open. To find out what another greater Egyptian gerbil is up to, TURN TO PAGE 26.

. . . a boomslang sunning himself near the road. To find out what another boomslang is up to, TURN TO PAGE 54.

. . . a white-headed duck paddling in the water. To find out what another white-headed duck is up to, TURN TO PAGE 15.

. . . a great white pelican chick that fell out of its nest. To find out what another great white pelican is up to, TURN TO PAGE 18.

. . . a purple swamphen chick that strayed too far from his mother. To find out what another purple swamphen is up to, TURN TO PAGE 52.

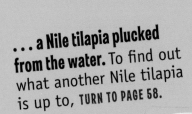

. . . a Nile tilapia plucked from the water. To find out what another Nile tilapia is up to, TURN TO PAGE 58.

. . . a greater flamingo chick newly hatched from its egg. To find out what another greater flamingo is up to, TURN TO PAGE 40.

. . . a newborn Nile crocodile that didn't stay near his mother. To find out what another Nile crocodile is up to, TURN TO PAGE 31.

A NILE RIVER FOOD WEB

In the Nile River, energy moves around the food chain from the sun to plants, from plants to plant eaters, and from animals to the creatures that eat them.

25

GREATER EGYPTIAN GERBIL *(Gerbillus pyramidum)*

The greater Egyptian gerbil's burrow is just yards away from the Nile River. But she has never been down to the water. She doesn't need to venture down. Gerbils drink very little water. She gets all the moisture she needs from the dew on the grass and from the food she eats.

Right now, the gerbil is moving her babies. Just two days old, they are tiny, hairless, and blind. Using her mouth, she picks one up by his tummy. She carries him to the new burrow she has dug out. Then she goes back for the other five. She'll move them a couple more times in the next few days, just to make sure predators won't find them.

Once she gets everyone settled, she sets to grooming them. She licks and licks, especially their rear ends. When they pee and poop, she licks that up too. After grooming, she carefully covers them with grass and sand. Then, as they nap, she sneaks out of her long tunnel.

First, it's time for a little bath of her own. But it's not a water bath. It's a dust bath. She rolls and fluffs her fur in the sand. Then her nose starts twitching. Its keen sense of smell is already picking up delicious scents from seeds, roots, and leaves waiting to be eaten.

Last night for dinner, the greater Egyptian gerbil nibbled . . .

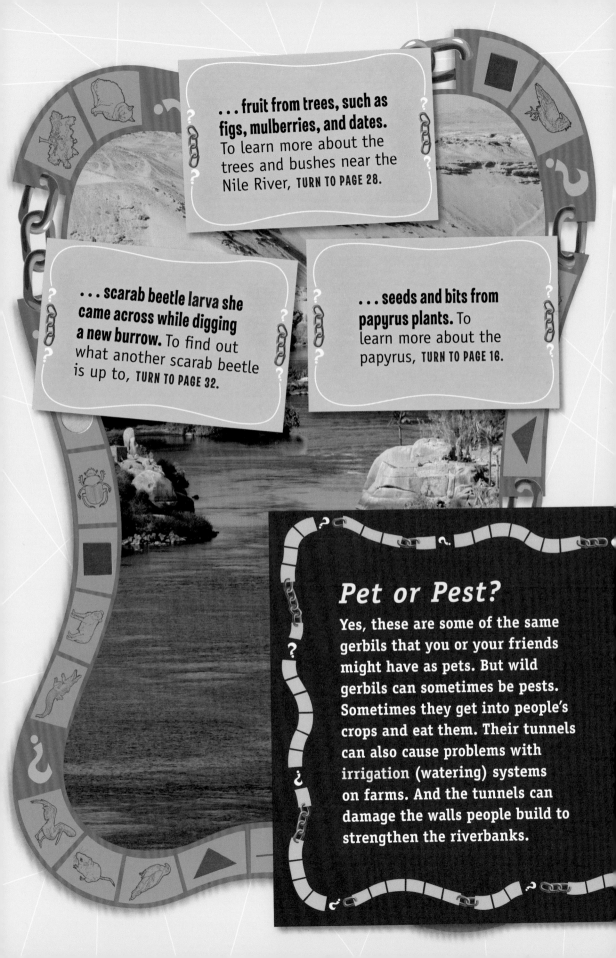

. . . fruit from trees, such as figs, mulberries, and dates. To learn more about the trees and bushes near the Nile River, TURN TO PAGE 28.

. . . scarab beetle larva she came across while digging a new burrow. To find out what another scarab beetle is up to, TURN TO PAGE 32.

. . . seeds and bits from papyrus plants. To learn more about the papyrus, TURN TO PAGE 16.

Pet or Pest?

Yes, these are some of the same gerbils that you or your friends might have as pets. But wild gerbils can sometimes be pests. Sometimes they get into people's crops and eat them. Their tunnels can also cause problems with irrigation (watering) systems on farms. And the tunnels can damage the walls people build to strengthen the riverbanks.

TREES AND BUSHES

The Nile River delta gets just a few inches of rain a year. So the trees and bushes must depend on the river for their water. In turn, the animals of the Nile River delta often depend on the trees for their survival. Trees such as sycamores grow tall and stately in the delta. They spread their branches wide and provide shade for animals that need a break from the hot sun. They also provide animals with cover from predators.

Many trees grow fruit. Mulberry bushes grow lower to the ground. Mulberries grow amid the bushes' oval leaves in the summer. These dark berries are eaten by many animals, including humans. Lotus trees and fig trees also provide fruit to those primary consumers looking for a sweet meal.

Farther out from the river, the land becomes more desertlike. The air is dry, and the soil is sandy. Trees such as the date palm take root in the shifting sand.

All these trees depend on the sun and carbon dioxide in the air to survive. They also need some amount of water, which they tap into underground with their roots. To grow, these trees need to take nutrients from the soil. These nutrients come from many sources, such as the decaying bodies of dead animals and poop from live animals. *Last night for dinner, the trees took nutrients from . . .*

sunlight

carbon dioxide

oxygen

Plants make food and oxygen through photosynthesis. Plants draw in carbon dioxide (a gas found in air) and water. Then they use the energy from sunlight to turn the carbon dioxide and water into their food.

29

A group of date palm trees are reflected in the Nile River.

. . . a dead and decaying **swamp cat.** To find out what another swamp cat is up to, TURN TO PAGE 8.

. . . **the poop of a golden jackal.** To find out what another golden jackal is up to, TURN TO PAGE 44.

. . . **the poop of a striped hyena.** To find out what another striped hyena is up to, TURN TO PAGE 12.

. . . **the poop of an Egyptian slit-faced bat.** To find out what another Egyptian slit-face bat is up to, TURN TO PAGE 37.

. . . a dead and decaying **boomslang.** To find out what another boomslang is up to, TURN TO PAGE 54.

. . . a dead and decaying **common reed frog.** To find out what another common reed frog is up to, TURN TO PAGE 47.

. . . **the poop of an Egyptian vulture.** To find out what another Egyptian vulture is up to, TURN TO PAGE 50.

NILE CROCODILE (*Crocodilus niloticus*)

31

Sorry, that's a log floating out in the river, not a Nile crocodile. This is a **DEAD END**.

Nile crocodiles used to live along the whole length of the Nile River. They even swam all the way out into the Mediterranean Sea. But then the Aswan High Dam was built in the 1960s. The wetland habitat of the delta region changed, and some of it disappeared. The crocodiles disappeared with it. You'll have to travel a distance upriver (south) before you'll get to see Nile crocodiles basking along the muddy shores of the Nile River.

SCARAB BEETLE (Kheper aegyptiorum)

The scarab beetle pauses in the long grass near the river. A smell drifts by—a bad smell. It would wrinkle your nose, but the odor is just what the scarab beetle is searching for. He flicks his long wings out from under his hard shell and takes off. He follows the breeze. There it is—a huge pile of dung (animal poop)! That's right. The scarab beetle actually seeks out dung. For this reason, the scarab beetle is also called the dung beetle.

The beetle gets right to work. He pats and prods the pile of dung. Soon he's got a small ball. Other beetles arrive. They pull and shape their own balls. There's plenty of dung to go around.

The beetle finishes smoothing out his ball. Now it's perfectly round. Just after he's done, a female lands near him. He rolls his dung ball toward her. She accepts the gift, and the two of them roll the ball off into the dusky night. They'll find a place to bury the dung ball so that the female can lay eggs in it.

Two scarab beetles roll a dung ball.

But before they get very far, they are ambushed! Another male tackles the ball and tries to roll it away from the pair. But it's two against one, and the pair wrestle the ball back. The ambusher scuttles off to pick on someone else.

Last night for dinner, the scarab beetle munched on . . . more dung. He can roll and bury up to 250 times his weight each night! He rolls, buries, and eats dung from a lot of different animals, such as . . .

. . . a golden jackal. To find out what another golden jackal is up to, TURN TO PAGE 44.

. . . a swamp cat. To find out what another swamp cat is up to, TURN TO PAGE 8.

. . . a Nile monitor. To find out what another Nile monitor is up to, TURN TO PAGE 34.

. . . a striped hyena. To find out what another striped hyena is up to, TURN TO PAGE 12.

More Than Just a Bug

Scarab beetles were important religious symbols in ancient Egypt. Egyptians believed the scarab was a lot like their sun god, Ra. Each day Ra would roll the sun across the sky and bury it each night, just like scarab beetles do with their dung balls. Because the scarab beetle was so important to them, Egyptians often used the image of scarab beetles in their decorations. They made scarab beetle necklaces and rings. They also gave friends and family scarab beetle amulets (special jewelry believed to bring good luck or to ward off evil).

NILE MONITOR *(Varanus niloticus)*

By the late afternoon, the Nile monitor needs some relief from the scorching sun. He waddles his body, 6 feet (2 meters) long, down toward the river. The air is cooler down there. He slips right into the water, diving down deep to see if there are any fish to be eaten. He can stay underwater for almost an hour. But this part of the river is empty. Even the fish have retreated to cooler, deeper water.

After a swim, the Nile monitor returns to the riverbank. He pads along until he comes across some soft, loose sand. Eagerly, the monitor flings the sand aside with his powerful front claws. Just down a few inches, he uncovers a nest of turtle eggs. He swallows some whole.

He still has a few eggs left when a golden jackal comes sniffing around. The monitor swells up his throat, opens his mouth, and hisses. He lashes his powerful tail at the jackal. The jackal yelps and leaps away. Only a starving animal would want to mess with a Nile monitor.

The monitor gulps down the last of the eggs in peace. As the sun sets, he heads back to a towering termite mound. His entrance has been clawed out of the side. He nestles himself in for a long night's sleep.

Last night for dinner, the Nile monitor swallowed . . .

. . . **snails from the edge of the river.** Lots of them. To find out what another snail is up to, TURN TO PAGE 48.

. . . **Egyptian tortoise eggs that were just buried.** To find out what another Egyptian tortoise is up to, TURN TO PAGE 51.

. . . **a greater flamingo chick wading in the water for the first time.** To find out what another greater flamingo is up to, TURN TO PAGE 40.

. . . **a common reed frog tadpole caught underwater.** To find out what another common reed frog is up to, TURN TO PAGE 47.

. . . **some great white pelican eggs left unattended just for a moment.** To find out what another great white pelican is up to, TURN TO PAGE 18.

. . . **a dead Nile tilapia that washed up onshore.** To find out what another Nile tilapia is up to, TURN TO PAGE 58.

. . . **a purple swamphen with a hurt foot.** To find out what another purple swamphen is up to, TURN TO PAGE 52.

. . . **some thrips in the dead weeds along the river.** To find out what other thrips are up to, TURN TO PAGE 42.

EGYPTIAN SLIT-FACED BAT *(Nycteris thebaica)*

The baby Egyptian slit-faced bat wakes up when his mother nuzzles him. It is dark in their cave. His giant ears—which are bigger than his head!—twitch with the sounds around him. He hears the stirring of other bats. And he hears the special call they make as they leave the cave. This cave is where they roost during the day. Now that it's night, they are leaving to go hunting.

After a couple of gentle nudges from her, he climbs aboard his mother. It'll be safer for him to come with her tonight as she hunts. If he stayed alone in the daytime roost, he'd risk getting caught by a predator.

The bats swoop out into the night. The mother bat heads to a favorite nighttime roost in a date palm tree. She grabs onto a twig and hangs upside down. The branch is smaller than your pinky finger, but it can hold the bats. Together, the mother and baby bat weigh less than a few coins. The mother bat listens with her giant ears. When she hears the sounds of a beetle down in the grass, she flaps off with her baby on board.

Echo, Echo, Echo...

All bats use echolocation. As they fly, they send out many sound signals, such as squeaks. The sounds bounce off objects such as the ground, trees, houses, and other animals. Bats can measure how long it takes the echo to bounce back to them. That tells them where the object is and how big it is. Bats use echolocation to avoid flying into things, even at night. But they can also use the echoes to hunt. The echoes tell them the size, shape, and location of nearby prey.

Egyptian slit-faced bats use echolocation. But the signals they send out are not very strong. Because of that, they are called "whispering" bats. And because their echolocation signals aren't strong, they rely on their sense of sight a lot more than other types of bats do.

As she gets closer to the beetle, she uses her echolocation to pinpoint the bug. She also has good eyesight and watches the ground carefully.

The baby bat holds tight. But as his mother turns quickly, he loses his grip on her fur. Suddenly, he is falling through the dark night!

The baby Egyptian slit-faced bat can't fly yet, so he falls to a pile of dead reeds near the river below. He's lucky that he didn't land in the river or that the fall wasn't any farther. He folds his wings around himself. All he can do is wait for his mother to find him—before someone else does.

Up above, his mother is using all her senses to try to find her baby on the ground. In moments she lands on the reeds next to him. She doesn't have to nudge him this time. He jumps on her body, and they're off the dangerous ground and in the air. She flaps back to the night roost. Hopefully their next hunting trip will be more successful.

Last night for dinner, the Egyptian slit-faced bat crunched on . . .

. . . a thrip in midflight. To find out what other thrips are up to, TURN TO PAGE 42.

. . . a scarab beetle scuttling for cover. To find out what another scarab beetle is up to, TURN TO PAGE 32.

GREATER FLAMINGO *(Phoenicopterus ruber)*

The greater flamingo is hard to miss on the Nile River. She's almost 4 feet (1.2 meters) tall and bright pink. She balances on one skinny leg, up to her knobby knee in the river's water. She lives within a **colony** (group) of flamingos. Sometimes colonies can have hundreds of thousands of members. This one has just a few hundred. But that's still a lot of flamingos. Around her, it is pink as far as she can see.

The flamingo stretches her long neck toward the water. She sticks her head right in and twists it upside down. Under the water, she sweeps her large bill back and forth along the bottom of the river. With quick tongue movements, she draws water in and out of her bill. Bristles along the edges of her beak strain the water. The water runs back out, but tiny shrimp, insect **larva**, snails, and plantlike life-forms called algae stay trapped in her mouth.

After about twenty-five seconds, she surfaces again. She takes a few steps, but the water quickly grows deeper. No problem. She just sits on the surface of the water, folds up her stick legs, and lets her wide webbed feet paddle her to where she wants to go down river.

Last night for dinner, the greater flamingo chewed on . . .

. . . snail larva from the bottom of the river. To find out what another snail is up to, TURN TO PAGE 48.

. . . tiny leeches just hatched from their water cocoon. To find out what other leeches are up to, TURN TO PAGE 20.

White Flamingos?

Flamingos are famous for their pink color. Did you know they get that color from the food they eat? The pink comes from all the brine shrimp (below) flamingos consume. The more shrimp they eat, the darker pink their feathers grow. Depending where flamingos live (and what their local diet is), they may be anywhere from hot pink to almost white.

THRIPS *(Thysanoptera)*

The thrip snuggles her long, oval body against the underside of a flower. Like all insects, she has six legs. She also sports short antennas and big, buglike eyes. She is just one of millions of thrips all over the world. There are more than five thousand kinds!

This thrip has just grown her wings. She has two sets, and they are both narrow and fringed. But her wings aren't the only way she gets around. As she picks her way along the smooth blossom, she uses her six short legs. These legs include a "balloon" near the feet that she can inflate or deflate. When inflated, it helps the thrip to stick to smooth surfaces—like this flower.

She crawls up the side of the flower. When she finds a good spot, she pierces the skin of the petal with her mouth. She sticks in her feeding tube and sucks up tiny bits of the petal's cells. Not all thrips eat live plants. Some live off the plants' **pollen**. And others eat dead plants and act as decomposers.

Last night for dinner, thrips in the Nile River area sucked on . . .

. . . **leaves and flowers from water lilies and lotuses.** To learn more about the water lilies and lotuses of the Nile, TURN TO PAGE 56.

. . . **dead leaves from a papyrus.** To learn more about the papyrus, TURN TO PAGE 16.

. . . **fruit and leaves from trees and bushes, both living and those dead on the ground.** To learn more about the trees and bushes near the Nile, TURN TO PAGE 28.

GOLDEN JACKAL (*Canis aureus*)

The golden jackal squats near the mulberry bush and lets out a spray of pee. There, that should let everyone know this is her family's territory. In the distance, she hears a howl. Her ears prick up. It's her mate. He is her partner for life. She tips her head back and howls in return. They "sing" together in the dusky night.

As they howl, they move toward each other. Then, as darkness falls, they begin to hunt. They keep their noses down to the ground. With a sniff, the female catches a whiff of a rabbit. She chases after it. Her mate waits. The female expertly drives the rabbit near him, and he launches himself at it for the kill.

As the two feast on the rabbit, they keep alert. Other animals are always nearby, ready to steal their meal. And sure enough, after a few mouthfuls, the male jackal growls at something out in the darkness. The female stops eating at once and begins clawing at the dirt next to their meal. Together, she and her mate dig a hole and push the rabbit into it. Then they push the dirt back over the rabbit.

Not a moment too soon. When they look up, another jackal stands in front of them. And this new jackal looks hungry.

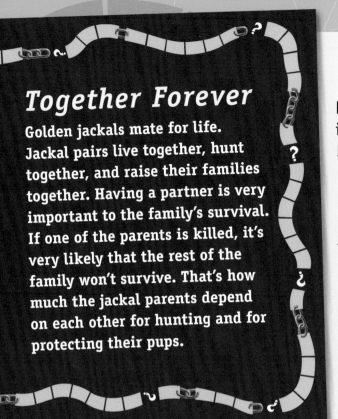

Together Forever

Golden jackals mate for life. Jackal pairs live together, hunt together, and raise their families together. Having a partner is very important to the family's survival. If one of the parents is killed, it's very likely that the rest of the family won't survive. That's how much the jackal parents depend on each other for hunting and for protecting their pups.

The new jackal doesn't hesitate. She barges right in and starts pawing at the buried rabbit. But instead of attacking her, the jackal pair greets her with yips and nose nuzzles. This jackal isn't a stranger. It's their grown daughter. Even though she's an adult, she still lives with her parents. She helps to care for the family's new pups. Next year she'll move out and find her own mate.

After the three finish off the rabbit, it's time to head back to the den.

The rest of the family waits there. No doubt they are as hungry as the adults were.

The three duck into the den, a narrow hole between two rocks near the river. Four tumbling, excited two-month-old pups wait for them. The adults haven't brought any of the rabbit back—at least not that you can see. But the pups nip and prod at the adults' mouths. Then each adult heaves up some of the rabbit they've eaten. The pups eagerly lick up the partially digested food. Just one more month and they'll be ready to start chewing their own solid food.

Last night for dinner, the golden jackals gulped down . . .

. . . **some figs from a fig tree.** Almost half of the jackals' diet is plants. To read more about the trees and bushes around the Nile, TURN TO PAGE 28.

. . . **a couple of white-headed duck eggs.** To find out what another white-headed duck is up to, TURN TO PAGE 15.

. . . **a scarab beetle pair scuttling along the ground.** To find out what another scarab beetle is up to, TURN TO PAGE 32.

. . . **an Egyptian slit-faced bat struggling with an injured wing.** To find out what another Egyptian slit-faced bat is up to, TURN TO PAGE 37.

. . . **a greater Egyptian gerbil tucking seeds in his cheeks.** To find out what another greater Egyptian gerbil is up to, TURN TO PAGE 26.

. . . **a young swamp cat whose mother had been killed.** To find out what another swamp cat is up to, TURN TO PAGE 8.

. . . **bits off a striped hyena that was hit by a car.** To find out what another striped hyena is up to, TURN TO PAGE 12.

. . . **a dead Nile crocodile.** To find out what another Nile crocodile is up to, TURN TO PAGE 31.

COMMON REED FROG *(Hyperolius viridiflavus)*

Sproing! The common reed frog leaps from a slender reed to a lily pad. She's just 1 inch (2.5 centimeters) long, so her landing barely makes a ripple on the river's surface. She hops to the edge of the lily pad and slips in the water. She has webbed feet at the ends of her long skinny legs. She uses those feet to push through the water.

She dives under the water lily. Underneath, along the lily's stem, she lays a wad of eggs. They look like a glob of lumpy, clear jelly. After making sure the eggs are snugly attached to the stem, she resurfaces. That's all she'll do as far as taking care of her babies.

After a few days, you'll be able to see tiny tadpoles growing in the eggs. Then they'll hatch and be able to swim on their own. Eventually, they'll grow arms and legs and lose their tails. Later in the year, they'll be ready to become parents themselves.

Meanwhile, the mother frog is off. She's found a swarm of flies and is busy lapping them up.

Last night for dinner, the common reed frog ate . . .

. . . newly hatched snails along the shore. To find out what another snail is up to, TURN TO PAGE 48.

. . . thrips hiding in the water lilies on the river. To find out what another thrip is up to, TURN TO PAGE 42.

. . . leeches squiggling in the shallows. To find out what other leeches are up to, TURN TO PAGE 20.

SNAIL *(Gastropoda)*

The snail flexes the muscular foot under his shell. The muscle ripples, and slowly the snail scoots along the stem of the reeds. As he moves, he leaves a trail of slime behind him. The snail makes the slime to help him move more easily.

Hundreds of kinds of snails live near the Nile River. The snail on the reed is a land snail and breathes air through a lung. The snail below him is a freshwater snail resting on the bottom of the river. He breathes through gills.

The freshwater snail slowly slides by a batch of snail eggs that are just hatching. The brand-new snails already have their shells, even though they are soft and transparent (see-through).

A shadow passes over the river bottom. A carp noses through the dead leaves. The fish gulps down the baby snails. The grown snail is knocked over in the water's movement. The snail draws in his foot and slams shut a little flap that covers his shell's opening. All he can do is drift in the water and wait to find out what happens.

Luckily, nothing picks him up and gobbles him down. The snail settles back down on the riverbed, sticks out his foot, and continues his journey.

Last night for dinner, the snail dined on . . .

. . . leaves and flowers from water lilies and lotuses. To learn more about the water lilies and lotuses of the Nile, TURN TO PAGE 56.

. . . papyrus stems. To learn more about the papyrus, TURN TO PAGE 16.

. . . fruit and leaves from trees. To learn more about the trees and bushes near the Nile, TURN TO PAGE 28.

Don't Forget the Calcium

Snail shells are made from a substance called calcium carbonate. As soon as snails are born, they need to eat calcium to strengthen their shells. Newborn snails will often eat the egg casing they hatched out of for their calcium. After that, snails have to find calcium in their food. If snails don't get enough, their shells will be thin and will break easily.

EGYPTIAN VULTURE (Neophron percnopterus)

The Egyptian vulture circles above the body of a dead cow. She's about the size of a chicken. Her small size means she'll have to wait for her meal. Bigger, stronger animals will eat first. Down below, hyenas and larger vultures rip into the carcass. When they are through, she'll wing in. Her smaller beak will snag the bits and pieces left behind.

But wait! She turns and banks. Maybe there's a quicker meal. She spots an ostrich pushing an egg out of its nest. An abandoned egg is one of her favorite snacks. She flaps down to the ground.

The egg is huge—the size of two dozen chicken eggs! She can't fit it in her mouth to crush it. And pecking it would do no good. Her beak would just bounce off the hard surface. But the vulture is a crafty one. She tries a trick she saw another Egyptian vulture do. She picks up a stone in her beak and bashes it into the egg. She hits the egg again and again, in the same spot, until the shell cracks. Then she slurps down the contents.

Egyptian vultures are one of the only birds in the world that use tools. But their clever ways may be disappearing because Egyptian vultures are disappearing. Their numbers have gone down quickly in recent years. In 2007 they were listed as being **endangered**. There isn't just one cause for their decline. They seem to be affected by fewer deer and antelope to eat and more power lines to tangle with.

But you know what that means—if they are endangered, this is a *DEAD END*. Turn back and pick another tertiary consumer.

EGYPTIAN TORTOISE *(Testudo kleinmanni)*

The small Egyptian tortoise pushes his way through the sand near the Nile River. He's the smallest tortoise in the world—about the size of the palm of your hand. His light tan color blends in with the sand around him, but it doesn't hide him completely. Someone is watching him. From the telephone pole above, a brown-necked raven swoops down and scoops up the tortoise for dinner. Unfortunately, that tortoise was the last one on the banks of the river. This is a **DEAD END**.

More and more often, Egyptian tortoises can't find a place to live. Human activity, such as farming and building, has destroyed the tortoises' habitat. And telephone poles and other structures have led new predators, such as the brown-necked raven, to the tortoise.

As a result, Egyptian tortoises are very **endangered**. If humans don't do something to help protect the tortoises, they will almost certainly become **extinct**. Only about 7,500 are left in the world.

PURPLE SWAMPHEN *(Porphyrio porphyrio)*

The young purple swamphen is about the size of a chicken. She wades in the marshy area of the river and pauses at a clump of reeds. She reaches out her left leg and grabs onto the stems with her foot. Then with her beak, she strips off the leaves and chomps them down.

She continues making her way through the thick weeds at the river's edge. Suddenly, a male pokes his black head through the reeds. He plucks a reed with his red beak and offers it to her. She hesitates. Then she takes the reed. The male swamphen bows and flaps excitedly. The two are now a pair.

They start scouting for the perfect place for their nest. Over the next few days, they build a platform of sticks and reeds right there in the shallow water. On the top of the nest, they create a shallow dip. This is where the female will lay three eggs.
As they finish off the nest, the male bends the tall reeds around the nest.

The bent reeds form a roof to protect them from sun, rain, and predators. *Last night for dinner, the purple swamphen picked up . . .*

. . . a crunchy snail or two. To find out what another snail is up to, **TURN TO PAGE 48.**

. . . **shoots and leaves from water lilies and lotuses in the river.** To learn more about the water lilies and lotuses of the Nile, **TURN TO PAGE 56.**

. . . **leaves from the papyrus plant along the river.** To learn more about the papyrus, **TURN TO PAGE 16.**

. . . **a common reed frog tadpole swimming through the dead leaves at the edge of the river.** To find out what another common reed frog is up to, **TURN TO PAGE 47.**

. . . **a leech scooped from the bottom of the river.** To find out what other leeches are up to, **TURN TO PAGE 20.**

. . . **some thrips taking a rest on the reeds.** To find out what other thrips are up to, **TURN TO PAGE 42.**

BOOMSLANG *(Dispholidus typus)*

The boomslang winds her body around the mulberry tree branch. This snake is about 3 feet (1 meter) long. Her name reflects her habitat. *Boom* mean "tree" and *slang* means "snake" in Afrikaans, a language spoken in South Africa.

Her greenish brown coloring makes her nearly invisible in the tree. She enjoys being able to see the river below without other animals spotting her. She rests. She watches with her huge eyes. And she waits for her food to come to her.

When a potential meal does come near—such as this dormouse scampering along the branch below—well, watch out! The boomslang inflates her neck. Then she strikes and grabs the mouse's head. The boomslang bites down. Fangs in the back of her mouth pierce the dormouse. A poison called **venom** flows through the fangs into the dormouse. The powerful venom kills the dormouse. After a few minutes, the boomslang stretches her mouth around the dormouse and swallows it whole.

The snake's body slowly begins to digest the dormouse. The boomslang won't need to eat for a while. She retreats up the tree to a favorite resting place—an old bird's nest.

Last night for dinner, the boomslang swallowed . . .

Immediate Attention Required

A boomslang's bite can be deadly to humans. It is particularly dangerous because several hours may pass before a person sees any symptoms. If that person thinks that the bite wasn't serious and waits too long to get medical attention, it may be too late. By then, the venom will have reached the victim's bloodstream. Traveling through the body, the poison will cause a headache and stomachache. Most seriously, it will cause the person to bleed on the inside.

In the 1950s, a famous snake scientist, Dr. Karl P. Schmidt, was killed by a boomslang. He was studying the snakes, and one of them bit him. He knew how deadly boomslang venom is, but he could not get medical help in time.

. . . a Nile monitor lizard hatchling warming itself in the sun. To find out what another Nile monitor lizard is up to, TURN TO PAGE 34.

. . . a common reed frog hiding in the wet leaves onshore. To find out what another common reed frog is up to, TURN TO PAGE 47.

. . . an Egyptian vulture egg stolen from its nest. To find out what another Egyptian vulture is up to, TURN TO PAGE 50.

. . . a newborn black kite that fell out of its nest. To find out what another black kite is up to, TURN TO PAGE 22.

. . . an Egyptian slit-faced bat roosting for the day. To find out what another Egyptian slit-faced bat is up to, TURN TO PAGE 37.

. . . a greater Egyptian gerbil searching for seeds. To find out what another greater Egyptian gerbil is up to, TURN TO PAGE 26.

WATER LILIES AND LOTUSES (Nelumbo nucifera)

In this quiet bend of the Nile River, the round pads of the lilies or lotuses are so thick, they carpet the water. And the pads are big—about the size of a dinner plate. It looks as if you could walk right across them. Of course, their round leaves are only floating on the surface and couldn't support you.

Actually, what you see floating on the water's surface is only part of the plant. Each leaf is tethered to the riverbed by a long, underground stem called a rhizome. These rhizomes grow roots in the bottom of the river. They then grow up to the surface where they sprout circular leaves, pink blossoms, and hard brown seeds.

The whole Nile River delta has been compared to a lotus blossom. If you look at it from the air, the Nile River looks like a long, slender rhizome. It spreads into a wide triangle shape as it runs into the Mediterranean Sea. That wide spot is called the lotus blossom.

Last night for dinner, the lilies and lotuses soaked up...

56

Left: A lotus
Right: A water lily blooms on the Nile River.

. . . **sunshine.** To learn how plants use sunshine, **TURN TO PAGE 28.**

. . . **nutrients in the riverbed's soil that came from poop from a purple swamphen.** To find out what another purple swamphen is up to, **TURN TO PAGE 52.**

. . . **nutrients in the riverbed's soil that came from a white-headed duck's poop.** To find out what another white-headed duck is up to, **TURN TO PAGE 15.**

. . . **nutrients in the riverbed's soil that came from decaying papyruses.** To learn more about the papyrus, **TURN TO PAGE 16.**

. . . **nutrients in the riverbed's soil that came from a Nile tilapia's poop.** To find out what another Nile tilapia is up to, **TURN TO PAGE 58.**

. . . **nutrients in the riverbed's soil that came from dead snails.** To find out what another snail is up to, **TURN TO PAGE 48.**

. . . **nutrients in the riverbed's soil that came from dead leeches.** To find out what other leeches are up to, **TURN TO PAGE 20.**

NILE TILAPIA *(Oreochromis niloticus)*

The male tilapia swims through the water with his fan-shaped tail. He swishes the tail over the nest he made. Inside the nest are jellylike eggs. After he fans the nest, the tilapia backs up and stands guard. The female who laid the eggs swoops in. She opens her wide mouth, sucks the eggs in, and swims off.

No, she hasn't eaten them. She's protecting them. She will keep the eggs safe in her mouth until they hatch. Meanwhile, the male will prepare his nest for another female to use.

A couple of weeks later, a hundred tiny baby fish, called fry, swim out of the female's mouth. They hover around their mother like a cloud. Right from the start, they begin munching on itty-bitty pieces of plants and dead material in the water.

The fry can find their own food, but that doesn't mean they are all alone. When a perch swims by, hungry for a bite to eat, the mother tilapia opens her mouth wide. Instantly, the fry swim in. The mother tilapia closes her mouth. One look at her and the perch swims away. At almost 5 pounds (2.3 kilograms), the tilapia is much larger than the perch. When the coast is clear, the mother lets her fry back out to eat and play. She'll continue to protect them until they get too big to fit in her mouth.

Last night for dinner, the Nile tilapia slurped down...

. . . leeches just hatched from their cocoon. To find out what other leeches are up to, TURN TO PAGE 20.

. . . bits of leaves and flowers from water lilies and lotuses. To learn more about the water lilies and lotuses of the Nile, TURN TO PAGE 56.

. . . snail larva floating in the river current. To find out what another snail is up to, TURN TO PAGE 48.

. . . a thrip that fell into the water. To find out what another thrip is up to, TURN TO PAGE 42.

. . . rotting seeds and stems from a papyrus plant. To learn more about the papyrus, TURN TO PAGE 16.

A Swimming Bug Killer

Tilapias are mostly primary consumers, or plant eaters. Adults are quite large—up to 11 pounds (5 kg). But despite their size, they don't bite off chunks from the plants of the rivers. Instead, they suck in the tiny bits of plants that float in the river. They also eat the other things that float in the water, such as insect larvas. Mosquitoes are an example of an insect that grows as a larva in the water. Mosquitoes carry diseases that kill thousands of people each year in Africa. So, many people welcome tilapia because they kill off the mosquito larvas.

GLOSSARY

calcium: a mineral that helps to grow strong bones and teeth

carcass: the dead body of an animal

carnivore: an animal that eats other animals

colony: a group of animals of one type that live together

decomposers: living things, such as insects or bacteria, that feed on dead plants and animals

delta: low ground between branches of the mouth of a river where rich soil is found because of the river deposits

echolocation: a method bats use to find food and to avoid flying into things

endangered: in danger of dying out

extinct: no longer existing

food chain: a system in which energy moves from the sun to plants and to animals as each eats and is eaten

food web: many food chains linked together

habitats: areas where a plant or animal naturally lives and grows

irrigation: a method watering land to help crops grow

larva: the wormlike stage in an insect's life between the egg and adult forms

nutrients: substances, especially in food, that help a plant or animal survive

pollen: powdery substance some plants produce and use to make seeds

predators: animals that hunt other animals for food

prey: animals that are hunted for food by other animals

primary consumers: animals that eat plants

producers: living things, such as plants, that make their own food

scavengers: animals that eat dead plants or animals

secondary consumers: animals and insects that eat other animals and insects

tertiary consumers: animals that eat other animals and that have few natural enemies

venom: poison used by snakes to defend themselves and to catch food

FURTHER READING AND WEBSITES

BOOKS

Cumming, David. *The Nile*. Milwaukee: World Almanac Library, 2003. Explore the history of the river and the environmental issues concerning it.

Day, Nancy. *Your Travel Guide to Ancient Egypt*. Minneapolis: Twenty-First Century Books, 2001. This Passport to History book takes readers back for a glimpse of daily life in ancient Egypt.

Kreb, Laurie. *We're Sailing Down the Nile: A Journey through Egypt*. Cambridge, MA: Barefoot Books, 2007. Follow a riverboat as it sails down the Nile.

Markle, Sandra. *Crocodiles*. Minneapolis: Carolrhoda Books, 2004. This book is part of the Animal Predators series. Other books in the series include *Hyenas* and *Vultures*.

Reynolds, Jeff. *Egypt: A to Z*. Danbury, CT: Children's Press, 2005. Reynolds offers an alphabetical tour of Egypt, featuring lots of animals.

Ryan, Patrick. *Welcome to Egypt*. Mankato, MN: Child's World, 2008. Learn more about the country of Egypt today, including the plants and animals of the Nile River.

WEBSITES

Ancient History Egyptians: Sacred Animals of Ancient Egypt Gallery
http://www.bbc.co.uk/history/ancient/egyptians/animal_gallery.shtml
On this BBC website, learn about the animals of the Nile River while you see them in artwork created thousands of years ago.

Egytomania Animals
http://www.clevelandart.org/kids/egypt/animals/
The Ancient Egyptians placed special value on the animals of the Nile. Find out more about these animals and what role they had in ancient Egyptian history and culture on this Cleveland Museum of Art website.

Wild Egypt: About the Animals of Egypt
http://touregypt.net/wildegypt
Take an online safari tour of the Nile and its creatures.

SELECTED BIBLIOGRAPHY

Burnie, David, and Don E. Wilson. *Animal: The Definitive Visual Guide to the World's Wildlife*. London: DK, 2005.

Collins, Robert O. *The Nile*. New Haven, CT: Yale University Press, 2002.

IUCN Species Survival Commission. *2007 IUCN Red List of Threatened Species*. N.d. http://www.iucnredlist.org/ (September 14, 2008).

McKay, George, ed. *The Encyclopedia of Animals: A Complete Visual Guide*. Berkeley: University of California Press, 2004.

National Audubon Society Field Guide to African Wildlife. New York: Alfred A. Knopf. 1995.

University of Michigan's Museum of Zoology. *Animal Diversity Web*. 1995–2008. http://animaldiversity.ummz.umich.edu/site/idex.html (September 15, 2008).

Williams, J. G., and N. Arlott. *A Field Guide to the Birds of East Africa*. London: Collins, 1980.

World Wildlife Fund. "Nile Delta Flooded Savanna." *worldwidelife.org*. 2001. http://www.worldwildlife.org/wildworld/profiles/terrestrial/pa/pa0904_full.html (September 15, 2008).

———. "Wildfinder." *worldwidelife.org*. 2008. http://www.worldwildlife.org/wildfinder/ (September 14, 2008).

INDEX

Photo Acknowledgments

The images in this book are used with the permission of: © Mark Harris/The Image Bank/Getty Images, background photographs on pp. 1, 4–5, 6–7, 11, 14, 17, 19, 21, 24, 27, 30, 33, 36, 39, 41, 43, 46, 49, 53, 55, 57, 59; © Juniors Bildarchiv/Photolibrary, p. 9; © Arco Images/Alamy, p. 10; © Terry Whittaker/FLPA, p. 12; © Anup Shah/naturepl.com, pp. 13, 44; © Eyal Bartov, pp. 15, 48, 50, 58; © DEA/G. DAGLI ORTI/Getty Images, p. 16; © Winfried Wisniewski/Minden Pictures, p. 18; © Biosphoto/Cordier Sylvain/Peter Arnold, Inc., p. 19 (inset); © INTERFOTO Pressebildagentur/Alamy, p. 20; © Bilagentur-online/McPhoto/Alamy, p. 22; © Federico Veronesi/Gallo Images/Getty Images, p. 23; © Sahara Nature-Fotolia.com, p. 26; © Wolfgang Kaehler/Alamy, p. 29; © Woodfall/Photoshot, p. 31; © Luke B. Barnett/naturepl.com, p. 32; © Panoramic Images/Getty Images, p. 34; © Penny Boyd/Alamy, p. 35; © Robert and Linda Mitchell, p. 37; © Michael Poliza/Gallo Images/Getty Images, p. 40; © Tom Adams/Visuals Unlimited, Inc., p. 41 (inset); © PREMAPHOTOS/naturepl.com, p. 42; © Barbara von Hoffmann/Animals Animals, p. 45; © Gerold & Cynthia Merker/Visuals Unlimited, Inc., p. 47; © Mike Nelson/epa/CORBIS, p. 51; © AfriPics.com/Alamy, p. 52; © WILDLIFE/Peter Arnold, Inc., p. 54; © Clinton Friedman/Gallo Images/Getty Images, p. 56 (left); © Jozsef Szentpeteri/National Geographic/Getty Images, p. 56 (right). Illustrations for game board and pieces © Bill Hauser/Independent Picture Service.

Cover: © Johnny Stockshooter/Alamy (background); © Anup Shah/Photodisc/Getty Images (left); © Kristian Sekulic/Dreamstime.com (second from left); © Cris Bouroncle/AFP/Getty Images (second from right); © ZenShui/Michele Constantini/PhotoAlto Agency RF Collections/Getty Images (right).

64

About the Authors

Don Wojahn and Becky Wojahn are school library media specialists by day and writers by night. Their natural habitat is the temperate forests of northwestern Wisconsin, where they share their den with two animal-loving sons and two big black dogs. The Wojahns are the authors of all twelve books in the Follow that Food Chain series.